THE HOW AND WHY WONDER BOOK OF
LIGHT AND COLOR

Written by Harold Joseph Highland, B.S., M.S., Ph.D. Associate Professor, Chairman of the Department of Business Administration, College of Business Administration, Long Island University.

Illustrated by George J. Zaffo

Editorial Production: Donald D. Wolf

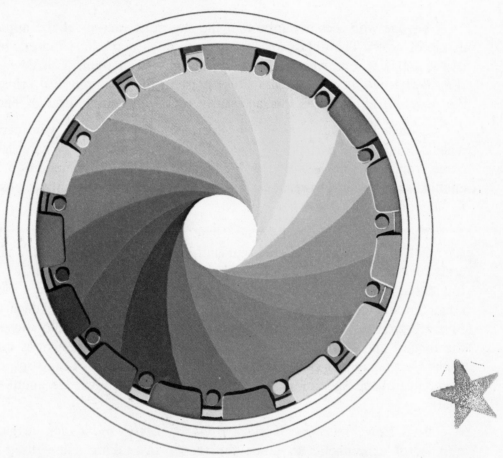

Edited under the supervision of
Dr. Paul E. Blackwood,
Washington, D. C.

Text and illustrations approved by
Oakes A. White, Brooklyn Children's Museum, Brooklyn, N. Y.

GROSSET & DUNLAP · Publishers · NEW YORK

Introduction

Anyone who sees a rainbow in the sky must marvel at the apparent magic of color. The appearance of a rainbow is marvelous indeed, but it is not magic to one who understands the nature of light. This *How and Why Wonder Book of Light and Color* presents the basic physical principles that explain the common characteristics of this essential form of energy.

Though light is a part of our experience day after day, who can say what it is? Is light particles of energy? Is it wave motion? Where does it come from and where does it go? Observation and experimentation have enabled scientists to answer these questions in part, but it is not yet possible to say conclusively just what light is.

There is great diversity everywhere in nature. One of the goals of scientists is to discover patterns that unify our understanding of the apparently unordered universe. In the study of light, for example, scientists have found that heat, X-rays, radio waves and cosmic rays all have a certain common characteristic. They all travel in a wave-like motion. When these rays are arranged according to the length of their waves, radio waves are the longest and cosmic rays are the shortest. This arrangement is known as the electromagnetic spectrum, and light is the visible part of this spectrum. Reference to this spectrum helps scientists organize knowledge about wave energy.

This *How and Why Wonder Book of Light and Color* suggests a number of experiments to guide the reader in making some discoveries about light and color for himself. It is a useful addition to every home or school library where there are potential young scientists at work.

Paul E. Blackwood

Dr. Blackwood is a professional employee in the U. S. Office of Education. This book was edited by him in his private capacity and no official support or endorsement by the Office of Education is intended or should be inferred.

Library of Congress Catalogue Card Number: 63-9530

Contents

The Nature of Light

Many many years ago, if we looked in a dictionary, we would find that light was described as the opposite of darkness. **What is light?** Today, scientists tell us that light is a form of energy that radiates or gives off rays just as a pebble creates waves if we dropped it into a pond of water. These rays, or light waves, as they are sometimes called, can travel through space and certain kinds of materials.

Light waves that reach and enter our eyes produce a sensation that we call sight. Light is our guide to the world around us. Because of light we can see our way around our homes; we can see to walk through streets; we can see the sky and we can even read this book. If you closed your eyes, you would not see this page because your eyelids would prevent the light rays from entering your eyes.

Thus, we have established one fact about light: unless the light from an object enters our eyes, we cannot see the object. Some objects, like the sun, stars and the electric bulb give off their own light. They radiate light because they are very hot, or as scientists call them, red-hot and white-hot bodies. The light waves they radiate are known as *incandescent light*. Most of the light we receive is from the largest source of incandescent light — the sun.

Another source of light is produced by electric sparks in tubes containing special gases; that is known as *fluorescent* or *cold light,* and we shall explore this type of light more fully later in this book.

The light we see directly from the source of light, such as the sun, an electric bulb or a fluorescent lamp, is known as *direct light*. If this light is reflected

or bounced off a surface in the same manner as a ball thrown against a wall, the light is known as *indirect* or *reflected light*. The light we see from the moon or the planets is an example of this type of light. It is light from the sun that has been reflected by the surface of the moon or that of the planets before it reaches our eyes.

Light is also a messenger of the universe. The light we see either directly from the sun and stars or indirectly from the moon and planets, tells us not only that they exist, but also enables us to determine their location.

Scientists have told us that light is a form of energy because it produces chemical changes in objects. The light that green plants receive helps the plants to make their food from water and carbon dioxide. We can see that without light, plants would not grow and there would be no food. Another example of chemical change produced by light takes place within every camera. The light striking the specially prepared chemical coating on the film produces

The "direct light" of the sun becomes "indirect light" as it reaches the dark and narrow street after being reflected by a window.

an image or picture on that film. Likewise, the light that strikes the special chemical coating of a photoelectric tube or cell combines with that chemical to produce an electric current.

Furthermore, without the sun's light warming the earth's surface, it would be so terribly cold that life could not exist. Without light, there would be no winds or rain. The winds are created by the sun's heating of the surface of the earth. Some areas of the earth become hotter than others; for example, the sunlight can warm desert sands more than it can the ocean, or warm the fields and city streets more than the icy regions at either the North or South Pole. The difference in temperature between any two heated areas of the earth will cause the air to flow and thus create winds. As the winds move over the earth, they pick up dust and other small particles and these combine with water that has evaporated when the sunlight heated the lakes, ponds, rivers and oceans. The small particles of water and dust form clouds that ride with the winds. Under certain temperature conditions, the water in these clouds is released, and it comes back to earth as rain or snow.

Thunderstorms have always been fascinating to man. In any **How does light travel?** such storm, you see the flash of lightning before you hear the thunder. You see the lightning because the light travels faster than the sound. Light travels about 186,200 miles per second and sound about 1100 feet per second.

At this tremendous speed, the light from the sun, which is about 93,000,000 miles away, takes about eight minutes to reach us on earth. It is possible for us to see 93,000,000 miles away. But if you went to the top of a high mountain or tall building, how far away could you see? Certainly you would not be able to see the Pacific Ocean if you were atop either the Rocky Mountains in Wyoming or the Empire State Building in New York.

You can see the sun but cannot see far across the earth's surface because light waves travel in straight lines. They cannot go around a corner or around an object.

Look at a man walking down a street or road in the sunlight **Why are there shadows?** and you will see his shadow. If you watch two men walking in the sunlight and carrying a six-foot pane of glass between them, you will see the shadow of each man six feet apart, but there will be no shadow of the pane of glass.

Shadows are easily explained since we know that light travels in a straight line. We also know that light waves pass through some bodies and not through others.

When light strikes a body and passes through it unchanged, we call such a body or material *transparent*. Most glass is such a material, especially window glass, and it is for this reason that we do not see the shadow of the window pane which the men are carrying. Do you know of any other transparent materials? The most common one, with which we are familiar, is air. Another is clear water.

On the other hand, some materials do not let light pass through them at all.

They stop the light waves just as you would catch a ball that was being thrown to someone standing behind you. Such materials are called *opaque*. Men's bodies, like steel, rock, concrete or even cardboard, are opaque and do not permit the light to pass through. An opaque body casts a shadow.

In addition to transparent and opaque

What materials scatter light?

materials, there is a third type of substance which is more like a transparent material than an opaque material. This type permits the light waves to pass through it, but unlike transparent materials, we cannot see through these materials. They scatter the light rays rather than permitting them to pass through unchanged.

These materials are known as *translucent*. Frosted glass, like that used for frosted light bulbs, is translucent. Other examples are very thin cloths or paper, such as waxed paper. Take a piece of waxed paper and hold it between you and a lighted electric lamp. You will see the light shining through the waxed paper, but you will be unable to see the lamp. This is because the waxed paper scatters the light. This scattering of light is known as *diffusion*.

When a light shines on an opaque ob-

Why do shadows vary in size?

ject, that object casts a shadow. Maybe you have noticed that sometimes your shadow is very big and other times it is small. When you are out in the sunlight at

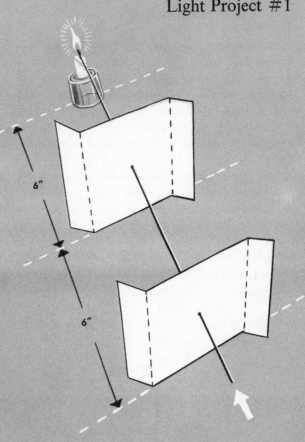

HOW TO DEMONSTRATE THAT LIGHT TRAVELS IN A STRAIGHT LINE

To do this experiment you need two large pieces of cardboard and a long straight wire or knitting needle and a candle.

Bend both pieces of cardboard as shown and make a small hole in each piece of cardboard. Punch the hole in both pieces of cardboard at the same time so that both holes are exactly in the same position on each piece.

Light the candle and line up both pieces of cardboard as shown in the sketch so that the first piece is six inches away from the candle and the second cardboard six inches from the first. Set the candle on a glass so that when you are looking through the small holes, you see the flame of the candle.

If you slip the knitting needle or wire through both holes, it will reach the flame of the candle; use a metal knitting needle so it won't burn and take it out of the flame quickly before the metal gets hot. The straight wire or needle is the path of the light.

Now if you remove the wire or needle and move the cardboard nearest you to one side or the other and again look through the holes, you will be unable to see the flame directly — proof that light travels in a straight line.

HOW TO EXPERIMENT WITH SHADOWS

Cut a circular disc of cardboard a little bit smaller than the size of the lens of a flashlight. Attach the cardboard to a short, thin stick. Stand about a foot away from any wall in a dark room so that your right side is facing the wall. Hold the flashlight in your left hand; turn it on and shine it at the wall. Now, in your right hand, hold the stick attached to the cardboard disc and place the disc about a foot away from the flashlight. The shadow of the cardboard on the wall is about the same size as the cardboard itself. Now cut a circular disc of cardboard about twice as large as the lens of the flashlight, and attach it to a thin stick. Stand in the same position with the wall on your right and the lighted flashlight in your left hand shining on the wall. Place the larger cardboard disc about a foot away from the light, between the flashlight and wall. Now you will notice that the shadow is much larger than the piece of cardboard.

If the object is larger than the light source, its shadow will be much larger than its real size. Similarly, an object smaller than the light source, at the same distance from the light, will cast a shadow much smaller than its real size, and an object of equal size at the same distance, will cast a shadow of equal size.

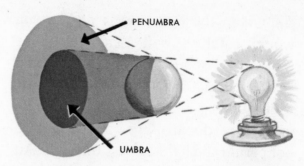

A tiny light ray, that would pass through a small hole in a cardboard, will produce a uniformly dark shadow when an opaque object is placed in its path. When the source of light is larger, however, such as an electric bulb, the sun, or even a candle, we often find multiple shadows. One shadow is dark and sharply defined, while the other is indistinct and blurry. The center or dark, sharp shadow is known as the *umbra*, caused when all of the light waves in this area are stopped. The blurry, indistinct shadow is known as the penumbra, and this lighter shadow is created because not all the light has been completely stopped by the opaque object.

Light Project #2

noontime, you will find that your shadow is small; but late in the afternoon, your shadow is much larger. Thus, we have one of the first rules about shadows: the size or length of the shadow depends upon the angle at which the light strikes the object. The size of the shadow is also influenced by the size of the source of light and the size of the opaque object.

Shadows used to help people tell the time of day before clocks were invented and even for a long while before clocks and watches were commonly used. They used a sundial to tell the time of day; in fact some people still use sundials but mainly for decoration in their gardens. The time of day was "read" from the sundial, just as we read time by looking at the hands of a clock. They could read the sundial either by the length of the shadow or the position of the shadow.

Hold this book close to a table lamp

Why do lights look dimmer far away?

and the pages will appear bright and easy to read. But as you walk away from the light, holding the book in your hand, the pages become dimmer and more difficult to read if there are no other lights in the room. The brightness of the page in the book is called *illumination* and it depends upon the amount of light reflected by the page.

Illumination depends upon both the brightness of the source of light and the distance between the light and the surface receiving the light. Scientists have a formula to express the relationship between the distance and amount of illumination. It is known as the "Law of Inverse Square."

According to this scientific rule, the amount of illumination decreases very quickly the farther we are from the source of light. For example, a book held *one* foot away from the light receives four times as much illumination

as a book held *two* feet away from the light. Four feet from the light, the illumination is only one-sixteenth the amount of light received one foot from the light.

In other words, if we wanted the same

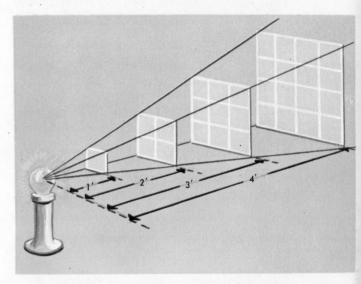

Illumination decreases very fast with distance.

amount of illumination on the book two feet from the light, as there was on the book one foot away, we would need a light that is four times as bright as the original light.

SUNDIAL

9

The Bending of Light

The image in the mirror shows right and left reversed.

Why are objects visible? The early Greek philosophers, some 3,000 years ago, believed that an object is visible to us because our eyes send out special rays, and that when these rays bounced off an object and returned to our eyes, we would see the object. Today, we know that our eyes do not send out the rays but instead receive the rays emitted by the object. We have already seen that these rays can be two types: (a) direct light, as we receive from a body that is a light source or generates its own light waves, such as the sun; and (b) indirect light, as we receive when a body reflects light, just as this page reflects the light by which we are reading. The body that produces its own light waves, like the sun or an electric bulb, is said to be *luminous,* while a body that reflects light, such as the moon or this page, is said to be illuminated. Thus, any object that sends light waves toward our eyes is visible.

How are light waves reflected? You have frequently seen your reflection in a mirror, on a polished table or in a window pane. These reflections exist because the light waves strike these surfaces and bounce off in much the same manner as a ball thrown against a wall.

While you would have little difficulty in distinguishing between your reflection and yourself when looking in a mirror, the scientist is careful to use specific terms or words to make this distinction. The reflection you see is known as a *reflected or mirror image,* while you or the actual object — a lamp in the room, a table, etc. — is referred to as the real object.

The mirror image or reflection we see, when looking into a mirror, is *symmetrical;* that is, everything facing the mirror appears to be repeated behind the mirror at the same distance as the original object is in front of it. Everything is the same, except for one thing: in the mirror image right and left are reversed. If you face a mirror and raise your right hand, the reflected image appears to raise its left hand.

How can we make light turn a corner? If you have already tried Light Project #1, page 7, you have proved for yourself that light travels in a straight line. We make use of this fact when we want to make light turn a corner. This is done by reflection.

The periscope, similar to that used in

10

a submarine or that used in a space capsule by an astronaut, makes use of the principle of reflection. Light is made to change its normal straight-line course by being reflected off a mirror or special surface. It is possible to control the direction of the reflected light because we know the "Law of Reflection."

According to this law or rule, if a light wave strikes a surface from which it will be reflected at an angle, it will "bounce off" at an angle. The light wave that strikes the surface is known as the *incident ray*. The angle between

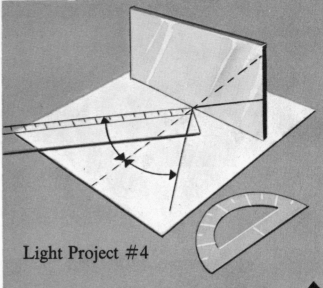

Light Project #4

HOW TO MEASURE THE ANGLE OF REFLECTION

We know that if we throw a ball straight at a wall, it will bounce straight back, and if we throw it at an angle, it will bounce off at an angle. This is known as the *Law of Reflection*. It also works for light.

All you need to test this law is: a mirror, a protractor, a pencil and a piece of paper.

1. Draw a dashed line on the paper and then draw a solid line to meet one end, so that they form an angle smaller than a right angle.
2. Take the mirror and place it at the point where the two lines join so that the dashed line on the paper and its reflection in the mirror appear as a continuous straight line.
3. Looking into the mirror, line up one edge of the ruler with the reflection of the solid line. Draw this line with your pencil.
4. Measure the angles on each side of the dashed line with the protractor. The two angles will be equal.
5. Try this several times, changing the size of the angle each time. The two angles will always be the same.

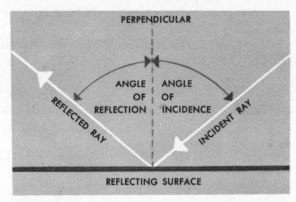

The angle of incidence equals the angle of reflection.

HOW TO DECODE "SECRET MESSAGES" WITH A MIRROR

As you remember from the previous section, mirror images are reversed. You can use this to decode "secret messages."

To write your message in code, place a piece of carbon paper, with the carbon side up, on the table and lay a piece of plain paper over it. Use the rounded edge of a toothpick or a pointed stick as a code "pencil." Write your message across the paper. You will see nothing on the top, but when you lift the paper, you will find that there is writing on the back of it.

To "decode" this secret message, you have to hold it in front of a mirror. Since the mirror reverses the image, the message is now as legible as if it were written the normal way.

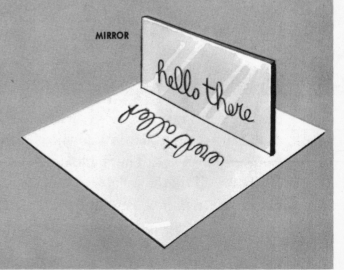

Light Project #3 ➡

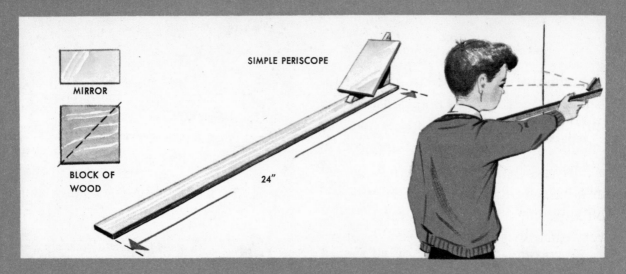

MIRROR

BLOCK OF WOOD

SIMPLE PERISCOPE

24"

Light Project #5   HOW TO MAKE A PERISCOPE

The simplest periscope requires only a small mirror, a stick about two feet long and a small block of wood. Cut the block so that each edge is as long as the mirror. Next, cut the block in half, cutting along a line joining diagonally opposite corners.

Attach half the block to the end of the stick and glue the mirror on the block as shown. You can now hold the stick and project the mirror section and see around a corner.

An enclosed periscope can be made by using two small mirrors, about 2 by 3 inches, the size ladies use in their handbags, and a piece of cardboard 8 inches wide and about 24 inches long. Measure off the distance shown in the diagram. Cut off the excess cardboard (shaded area); cut two one-inch circles as shown; then bend the rest of the board along the drawn lines.

The mirrors are held in place with cellophane tape and all of the edges of the periscope are also held together with cellophane tape.

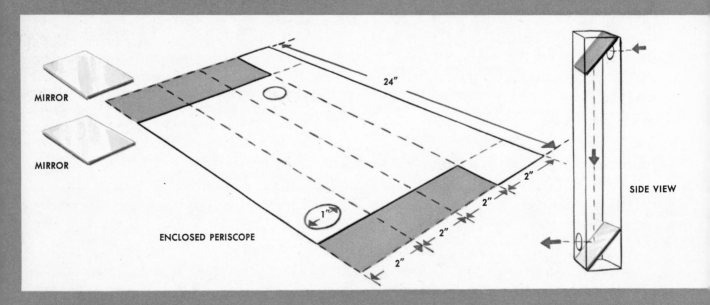

MIRROR

MIRROR

24"

2"

2"

2"

2"

1"

SIDE VIEW

ENCLOSED PERISCOPE

the incident ray and a perpendicular drawn to the surface is known as the *angle of incidence*. The light wave that has bounced off the reflecting surface is called the *reflected ray* and the angle between this ray-and the perpendicular is known as the *angle of reflection*. In every case, the angle of incidence is equal to the angle of reflection, as you can see when you try Light Project #4, "How to measure the angle of reflection," on this page.

The Law of Reflection is true under all conditions, whether the surface is smooth, like a mirror, or rough, like a sandy beach or a brick wall. If you took a flashlight on a moonless night and pointed it at a very smooth varnished wood exterior wall of a house, the light would be reflected. If the light were aimed at an angle to the wall, the angle of incidence would be equal to the angle of reflection.

What is diffused reflection?

However, when light strikes a rough surface, the light is diffused. The reason the light from a flashlight would not bounce off a rough brick wall as it did from a smooth wood wall, is that the light is sent off in different directions by the uneven surface. Yet, if we could examine each minute portion of the light — break the beam up into many individual light waves — we would find that in each case the law of reflection worked. But because the surface is made up of many small portions at different angles, each small light wave is reflected in a different direction.

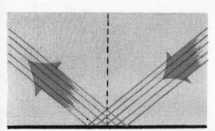

If light strikes a smooth surface, the reflection is regular.

If light strikes a rough surface the reflection will be diffused.

Why does light bend in transparent materials?

As you remember, we noted at the beginning of this book, that light waves travel through space and certain kinds of materials.

You observe refraction when you see a spoon or a straw in a glass of water. When you go spear fishing, you have to calculate the same refraction or you may miss your target.

We also found that when light waves go through a material, we say that the material is transparent. But light does not travel at the same speed through all materials; it goes slower through some than through others.

While light waves travel the most quickly through air, they go much slower through water and even slower through glass. When the light waves, traveling through the air, strike water or glass at an angle, they bend as they slow down. Scientists describe this bending by saying: "when light passes from one transparent medium (such as air,

13

water or glass) to another at an angle, the light waves are bent at the boundary between the two mediums." This bending is known as *refraction*.

You can see this easily if you put a straw in a transparent glass of water. The straw appears to be bent at the point where it enters the water.

This bending or refraction takes place every time the light wave passes from one medium to the next as long as the light passes the boundary between the two mediums at an angle. It takes place when light passes from the air into glass, and it takes place again when the light waves pass from the glass into the air. Refraction also takes place between air and water, water and air, water and glass, and glass and water.

What happens to light in hot moist air? There is always some moisture in the atmosphere, but when this amount increases substantially, it affects the light waves. Light traveling through space goes at a much faster speed than light waves passing through very moist air near the surface of the earth. Space and moist air are considered by scientists as two different mediums, just as water and glass are different. And just as light waves are refracted as they pass from air into glass or water, the light waves from space are refracted when they pass through the moist air.

You can see this refraction at work if you watch the sun setting on a very humid, warm day. Just as the sun nears the horizon, the previously round disk seems to have a flattened bottom; it is not a perfect circle. The light waves

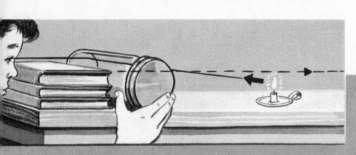

HOW TO PROVE THAT THE AIR BENDS SUNLIGHT

In the morning we actually see the sun before it comes over the horizon and in the evening, we see the sun after it has passed below the horizon. This is another example of refraction since the air around the earth bends the rays of the sun and makes us see the sun where it isn't located. You can try an experiment in your own home to see how this works. All you need is a large jar with a cover, a candle and several books.

Set the empty jar on its side and place several books one atop the other next to the jar until they are about two-thirds as high as the jar. Now take the books and place them along one edge of a table.

Light Project #6

About 24 inches from the same edge, place a very short candle in a dish or holder; the candle should be about half as high as the pile of books.

Fill the jar with water and put the cap on tightly. Now light the candle and you are ready to see how the air bends the sun's rays. The candle represents the sun and the jar of water is the air around the earth.

If you bend down so that you can look just even with the top of the books, you should be unable to see the flame on the candle. (If you do, shorten the candle.) Now, set the jar on its side alongside the books, between the books and the candle. If you sight along the top edge of the books, you will now be able to see the flame of the candle. The water in the jar has bent the light waves from the candle's flame toward you, just as the atmosphere bends the light waves from the sun before they reach your eyes.

coming from the bottom portion of the sun are refracted by the moisture in the air to create this optical illusion.

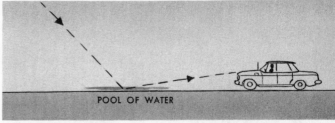

Frequently, when you are driving along

Why does a dry road look wet?

a turnpike or thruway on a clear, hot day, you see what appear to be pools of water on the highway up ahead. However, as you come closer, you find that the road surface that seemed wet before is actually dry. If you look ahead, there are the pools of water again; they seem to be moving in the same direction as the car.

Actually, there are no pools of water on the road at all. Those watery images are an illusion, a mirage, such as occurs in the desert or even on the water of a large lake or the ocean.

These pools of water, or any mirage for that matter, occur only under certain conditions. First, it is necessary to have a relatively flat surface, such as a roadway, water or sand. Secondly, you must be able to see a considerable distance over the flat surface.

Most important is the presence of a layer of hot, moist air on an otherwise perfectly clear day. This hot moisture-ladened layer of air immediately over the surface acts like a reflective surface, just as calm water does on a pond. Thus, as we look in the distance at a roadway, we will see the sky reflected by the layer immediately above the road. The reflection of the sky will make that portion of the roadway appear different from the other portions of the road; it will look like small pools of water.

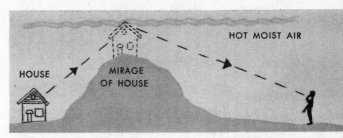

The pools of water you see in the road ahead on a sunny day disappear as you come close to them.

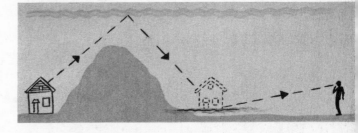

Single mirages (above) and double mirages (below) have fooled many travelers in the desert but are not limited to this location.

Sometimes, because of wind currents and air masses, a hot moist layer of air can be overhead. It may be exceedingly thin or it can extend upwards for a number of miles. The most important thing is that the air nearest the ground is cooler than that higher up. In this case, the hot layer again can act as a reflective surface. Light from a source many miles away can be reflected downward, causing a person on the ground to see what is commonly known as a mirage.

15

WHY DOES THE MOON LOOK BIGGER WHEN IT RISES?   Light Project #7

When we watch the moon come over the horizon, it often appears enormously large, only to become smaller and smaller as it rises in the sky and passes overhead. This is sometimes caused by refraction in much the same way as the sun appears to be flattening when it sets.

On warm moist nights, the air with the water in it causes the light from the moon to be refracted. The light waves bend as they pass through the moist air and produce one of the many optical illusions that our eyes play on us.

The illusion is most obvious when the moon is close to the surface of the earth or near the horizon; we see it behind tall trees or buildings and we are able to make a size comparison. Our eyes are unable to adjust for the true distance of the moon

from the trees and buildings and we make our comparison as if the moon were merely a little way behind the trees. The thousands of miles to the moon are compressed by our eyes. However, after the moon rises, we have no object with which to compare its size.

Nevertheless, you can satisfy your own curiosity as a scientist by "measuring" the moon as it comes over the horizon and as it climbs high into the sky. Take a clear piece of plastic and hold it at arm's length between your eyes and the moon. Mark the plastic in crayon so that you have a circle the same size as the image of the moon. Later, when the moon is high in the heaven, view the moon again through the plastic. You will be surprised to see that the circle you drew before is still just the size of the image of the moon.

16

Magic with Light

For ages magicians have fascinated audiences by putting the laws of reflection and refraction to use. The famous carnival magic trick of making a performer's head appear on a table while the rest of his body "disappears," is possible because of the magic that can be performed by light.

How can you make things invisible?

Let's review the basic idea of refraction so that we can understand how it is done. Remember that light waves leaving one medium and striking another at an angle, will bend as they travel through the second medium; that is, they will still travel in a straight line but in a direction different from the original one. Thus, when light passing through air enters water at an angle, the light wave will bend. Similarly, if that light wave completes its journey through the water and re-enters the air, that light wave will again change its direction because it bends as it passes from one medium to the next.

Thus, we can try some magic by putting a penny in the center at the bottom of a large opaque bowl. Look across the top edge of the bowl so that you cannot see the penny. While you stay in this position, have someone pour water into the bowl. Suddenly, as if by magic, you can see the coin which you could not see before. You see it because of the refraction of light.

But we started out to make things invisible, didn't we? Well, this previous trick was reverse magic—making something visible which wasn't visible, by using the bending of light waves. Now, let's make something invisible. This time we again place a penny in the center at the bottom of a large bowl, and we add water to the bowl at once.

If you look straight down into the bowl, you'll see the penny. Now start to move your head lower by bending your knees so that your eyes will eventually be looking over the edge of the bowl. As you move your head lower and still look at the penny, that penny appears to be moving. The penny looks as if it is climbing up the other side of the bowl. Then suddenly, as you're bending your knees more and more, the penny "disappears;" it looks as if it climbed out of the bowl and vanished in the air.

HOW TO MAKE A GLASS ROD VANISH

Another trick with light involves the use of a white-enameled funnel. Drill a small hole, ⅛ inch in diameter about halfway down from the top. Insert a clear glass rod, such as a drink mixer, through the narrow end of the funnel so that it projects about one-third the way into the funnel.

Hold the funnel and glass rod directly below a bright ceiling light. Peek through the small hole in the side. The overhead light will be reflected within the funnel and the glass rod will be invisible.

Light Project # 8

Actually, as you move your eyes lower toward the edge of the bowl, the angle of refraction increases. It finally reaches a point where the surface of the water acts as a reflector, or just like a mirror, so that it is no longer possible to see the penny. This particular angle, the one at which the penny disappears from view, is known as the *critical angle*.

Have you ever watched a movie or a television show where the wheels of a speeding automobile or an airplane taking off appear to be turning backward?

Why do forward moving wheels sometimes appear to be turning backward?

To understand this strange optical effect, you must realize that a motion picture film projected on the screen consists of a series of individual pictures. The pictures are joined together so that you can see one after another, but there is a very small time, a fraction of a second, between each frame or picture when the screen is completely dark.

Each individual picture shows the au-

tomobile or airplane moving along the road or the airfield. However, if the wheel does not make a complete turn from one still picture to the next, it looks as if the wheel is moving backward. For example, if we watch the top edge of the wheel in one picture and if that top edge does not make a complete turn, but instead completes three-

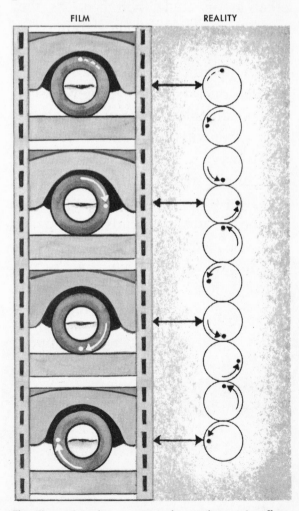

FILM   REALITY

The illustration demonstrates the stroboscopic effect.

18

fourths of a turn, it looks as if the wheel turned one-fourth backward. Now, in the third picture, with the wheel making only three-fourths of a turn, the top edge visible in the first picture is directly on the bottom. Again it appears as if the wheel has turned one-fourth backward. Thus, the automobile continues moving forward and wheels continue to appear to be going backward. This is known as the *stroboscopic effect*.

You can see this stroboscopic effect by using the accompanying diagram of the six concentric circles with the white

The wheels will turn!

gear in the middle. Hold the illustration at about arm's length away from you and concentrate on the circles. Hold one hand still and with the other shift the book up and down vertically, about two or three inches in each direction. Notice that the inside of the circles appears to be turning.

Have you noticed anything else? Yes? The gear inside the group of circles appears to be turning in the opposite direction of the circles. This is the same effect as we see when watching a car or train on the movie screen. It is the stroboscopic effect once again.

HOW TO MAKE A STROBOSCOPE

You can test the stroboscopic effect of light by making a simple stroboscope using a piece of cardboard four inches square and a small hand drill.

Cut the cardboard into a circle four inches in diameter. Divide the circle into eight equal pie-shaped sections. You can do this by drawing a line through the center of the circle and then drawing another at right angles through it; this divides the circle into four parts. If you divide each fourth into halves, you will have eight sections. Leave one section white and color the next, until you have four white sections and four colored sections.

Force a nail through the center of the circle so that the cardboard cannot turn unless you turn the nail. Insert the nail into the chuck of the drill. Now, holding the drill so that the circle faces you, turn the handle of the drill.

Because there are many types of hand drills, it is not possible to tell you exactly how fast to turn the handle. Try turning at varying speeds until you find the speed at which it will appear as if the disc is standing perfectly still.

Once you have found this speed, you will find that if you turn the handle just a little bit slower, the segments of the disc will appear to be turning backwards. Then as you increase the speed, the segments will appear to be standing still, and finally, as you turn even faster, the segments will move forward rapidly.

Light Project # 9

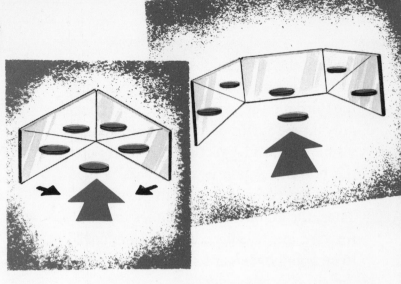

MULTIPLE IMAGES

The smaller the angle of the two mirrors becomes or when a third mirror is used, the faster the money "grows."

Every time light waves are reflected, we produce another reflected or mirror image. If you

How are multiple images created?

have ever been in a store where they have three mirrors so that you can see how you look in a new suit or dress, you will find that you can see three images of yourself and some times even more, depending upon the angle at which you look into the mirrors. You can use mirrors to "make money grow." Try this with only one penny and two mirrors, such as those used in a pocketbook.

Place the penny on a table and hold the two mirrors edge to edge so that all you see is a single reflection. Now, keeping the touching edges together, move the outside edges of both mirrors toward you. The closer the mirrors come together, the more images or reflections of the penny you see.

At first, you see a reflection of the penny in each mirror; then as the mirrors reflect into each other, you see four reflections plus the original penny—you now see five pennies. Now keep turning the mirrors, making sure that the touching edges are together, and that the outside edges practically touch the penny. Then you will see six reflections plus the real penny.

Lenses and Optics

Just a few pages ago, we saw how we could make things invisible by refracting or reflecting light waves. The refracting

What is a lens?

of light waves as they pass from one substance to another—from air to glass and then again from glass to air—helps us make objects appear bigger or closer than they really are, or can help us make objects appear farther away.

To do this we use lenses. A lens is a curved piece of glass that is used to

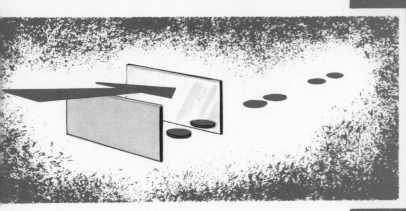

The number of images becomes infinite when the two mirrors face each other and are parallel to each other.

refract light waves, either concentrating them or dispersing the waves, depending upon the shape of the glass. While lenses have been made of glass for several centuries, today we also use special clear plastic to make lenses since the plastic lenses do not break as easily as those made of glass.

Essentially, there are three basic forms or shapes of lenses, although you will find many variations of each and, at times, even a combination of the basic shapes.

How are lenses shaped?

The *prism* or triangular shaped piece of glass is one form of a lens. If you look at this lens from its side, it would be shaped somewhat like a wedge of pie.

Another basic shape of a lens is *convex*. A side view of such a lens would reveal that it is thicker at its center than at its edge. If you picture two parentheses, such as ( ), so that they are in their proper order as we would use them when writing, you would have the shape of a convex lens by joining the tops.

The third basic shape of a lens is *concave*. When viewed from its side, this

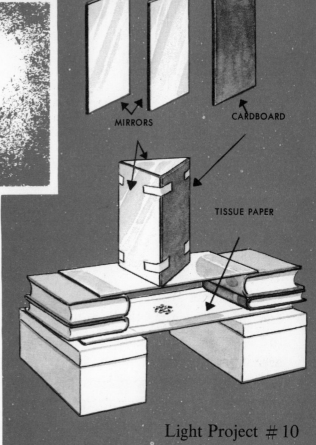

MIRRORS   CARDBOARD

TISSUE PAPER

Light Project # 10

HOW TO MAKE A KALEIDOSCOPE

For centuries, people have been fascinated by the kaleidoscope. The word means "beautiful form" in old Greek. It is a simple device to make multiple images.

To make one yourself, you need two mirrors exactly the same shape and size and a piece of cardboard to match. Stand the mirrors and the cardboard on their shorter edges in the form of a triangle with the mirrors facing the inside. You can hold the three pieces together with rubber bands or cellophane tape; cut a small piece of waxed paper to fit over one end and tape it into position.

Cut some very small pieces of colored tissue paper about the size of a pencil eraser, or you can use small chips of transparent colored plastic or glass. Set these on a piece of glass about ten inches above the table top; you can rest the glass on books or boxes. Use a shiny surface table or place an electric light under the glass.

Holding the mirror and cardboard triangle about two inches above the colored tissue or glass, look down through the top. You will see the many reflections of these small pieces. Actually, you will see six reflections plus the original of each little piece on the sheet of glass. By moving the small particles around on the glass, you can create many different patterns.

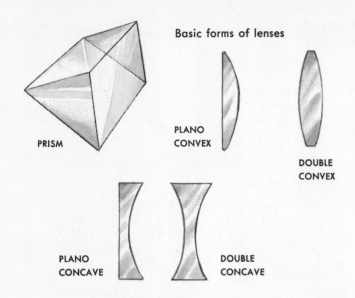

Basic forms of lenses

PRISM

PLANO CONVEX

DOUBLE CONVEX

PLANO CONCAVE

DOUBLE CONCAVE

lens is thinner at its center than at either end. If you picture two parentheses in the opposite way from that which they are normally used, such as)(, you would have the shape of a concave lens.

In studying lenses and how they refract light, it is best to review the path of a light wave as it passes through a piece of

How does light pass through a prism?

The path of light striking a windowpane at an angle and perpendicular.

LIGHT RAY PERPENDICULAR

GLASS

ORIGINAL PATH

LIGHT RAY AT AN ANGLE

GLASS

LIGHT RAY DISPLACED

glass, such as a window pane. The light wave may take either of two paths depending upon the angle at which it strikes the flat piece of glass.

If the light wave strikes perpendicular to the surface of the glass, that is at right angles to the surface, then the wave will pass through the glass unchanged. However, if the light wave strikes the glass' surface at an angle, it will be refracted. First, it is refracted as it passes from the air into the glass, that is, its direction is changed. Secondly, when the light wave leaves the glass and passes into the air, it is again refracted. Actually, the light will pass through the glass, coming out at the same angle at which it entered, but the path will be shifted over slightly. This shift in position of the path is known as *displacement*.

Similarly, when a light wave enters and leaves a prism, it is refracted. Let's trace the light wave's path since its refraction in a prism will help you to understand how light passes through the other two types of lenses as well.

First, let us consider the prism itself. A prism is usually a solid piece of glass, shaped as though you had taken a triangle and extended it backwards. In other words, a prism has two triangular bases at each end, and the three sides between the bases have the form of parallelograms. For purposes of a diagram, however, it is only necessary to see a triangle, which is actually a cross section of the prism. A wave can strike the prism either perpendicular to one of the sides or at an angle.

If the light wave strikes perpendicular

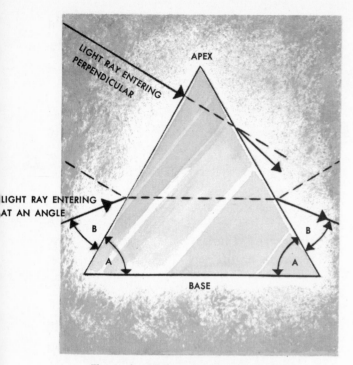

The path of light going through a prism.

How does light pass through convex and concave lenses?

If we look at a concave or convex lens from its side, we can draw an imaginary line from the top to bottom of the lens; this is known as the *axis* of the lens. At right angles to this axis and passing through the exact center of the lens is another imaginary line, known as the *principal axis*. In addition, any imaginary line we draw at any angle to the lens that passes through the center of the lens is known as the *secondary axis*.

Scientists have found that any light

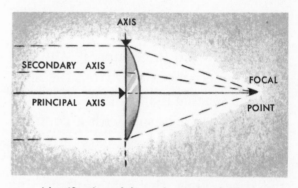

Identification of the major parts of a lens.

to the side, it will continue in the same path until it reaches the other side of the prism just before it is ready to pass from the glass into the air. At this point it is emerging at an angle to the air. Because it is striking the air at an angle, it will be refracted or bent.

On the other hand, if the light wave strikes the side at an angle, it will be refracted as it enters the glass. When it emerges on the other side of the prism — as it passes from the glass into the air — it is striking the air at an angle and will again be refracted. Scientists have found that the path at which the light wave leaves the prism is at the same angle with the base as the angle of the path at which it entered. Therefore, by knowing the angle at which the light wave will strike the prism, it is possible to determine the exact path at which it will leave.

wave traveling along either the principal axis or any secondary axis of a lens, passes through the lens unchanged; its path is continued without interruption. However, any light wave that strikes the lens along any other path is reflected by the lens.

Actually, more than one light wave originates from any object, just as a pebble dropped in a pond creates more than one wave in the water.

This is true whether the object is luminous, that is, the originating light source like a light bulb, or illuminated,

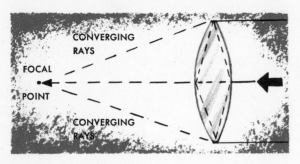

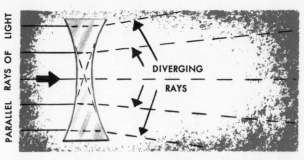

PARALLEL RAYS OF LIGHT

that is, reflecting light from a light source like this page of the book.

Let us examine what happens to these light waves that strike a lens along any path other than the principal or secondary axis.

The convex lens is also known as a *converging lens* since the light waves that pass through it converge or bunch together toward the center. If you look at a simple convex lens from the side, you will see that it appears to be a modification of two prisms with a common base. As the light waves pass through a prism, they are bent or refracted toward the base. Thus, the light rays passing through the top and bottom imaginary prisms of a convex lens are bent toward the center or converge.

Similarly, a simple concave lens can be regarded as a combination of two prisms which are joined at their tops or apexes. Since the light waves passing through a prism are refracted toward the base, we can see that the concave lens spreads the light waves away from its center. This bending outward of light rays is known as *divergence*.

How does a lens form an image?

If you hold a piece of paper in one hand and an ordinary reading glass (a convex lens) in the other so that the glass is between a window and the paper, you will see an *image* of the outside scene on the paper. As you move the reading glass closer or farther away from the paper, you will find that the image is clearest at one specific distance. When the image is clearest, the distance from the reading

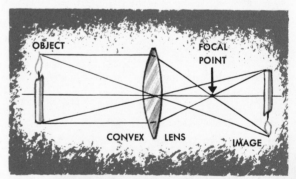

A simple reading glass can bring the "outside" into your room.

glass to the paper is the *focal length* of the lens.

This moving of the reading glass (lens) back and forth to obtain the sharpest possible image is exactly what we do when we focus a camera. We move the lens of the camera back and forth so that it will produce the sharpest image on the film.

You will notice something unusual about the image produced by the reading glass on the paper you are holding. It is upside down. The reason for this is that the lens *inverts* the scene when it produces an image, as is illustrated in the accompanying diagram.

How does science use lenses?

Without the use of lenses many great scientific discoveries and much of our scientific knowledge would not be possible. We use lenses in optical instruments, such as the microscope and telescope, to refract light and make objects appear larger than they do to the unaided eye. A microscope makes visible objects which the

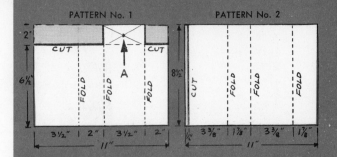

Light Project # 11

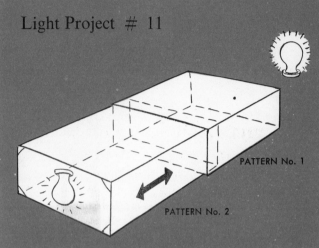

HOW TO MAKE A CAMERA OBSCURA

A very small pinhole acts the same as a convex lens and produces an inverted image. You can make a pinhole camera, also known as a camera obscura, with the following materials:

> Two pieces of heavy cardboard, each about 8½ x 11 inches;
>
> Some masking tape or cellophane tape;
>
> a piece of household waxed paper or tracing paper about 3 x 4 inches.

To make the camera, cut one piece of cardboard following pattern #1. Make a very small pinhole — the sharp end of a safety pin should be adequate — at point "A" in the diagram. Fold along the lines indicated and tape the edges together carefully with cellophane or masking tape. Make certain that the edges are tightly sealed so that no light can enter.

Now, cut the other piece of cardboard following pattern #2. Fold along the lines indicated and join with tape. Cut the waxed paper so that it fits over one end of this part of the camera, leaving a very small triangle open at each edge and tape it.

To use the camera, insert the part with the waxed paper end into the part in which you made the pinhole as shown; hold the waxed paper part close to your eyes, staying in a shady place outdoors, or if you are inside the house, stay away from direct sunlight. Aim the pinhole at a light or bright, sunny place. Move the inside portion of your camera back and forth slowly until the scene appears sharply on the waxed paper screen.

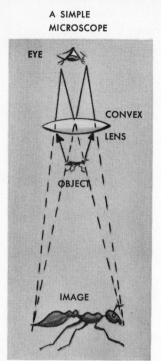

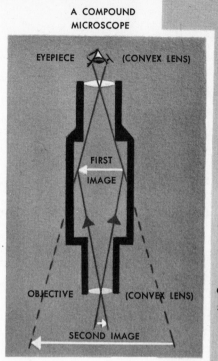

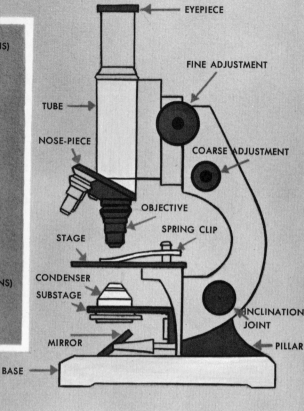

Without the use of lenses many discoveries made with the help of the microscope would not have been possible, because there would not be a microscope.

eye could not ordinarily see. We are able to study blood cells and minute plant and animal life, such as bacteria, and thus combat disease.

Lenses are also used in our study of space and the universe. The telescope brings distant stars and planets closer to earth by making them appear larger than they do to the naked eye.

Generally, several lenses, and often different types of lenses are used in combination in these scientific instruments. When we use only a single lens, such as a reading glass, we refer to the glass as a simple lens. When we use two or more lenses, the optical instrument is called "compound." A compound microscope is illustrated here.

By using several lenses to refract the light, it is possible to enlarge an object many many times. Modern optical mi-

croscopes can enlarge an object up to 2,400 times. A single period (.) on this page magnified that many times would appear to be the size of a disk with a 10-foot diameter.

If you have tried to obtain an image of an outdoor scene using the reading glass and plain paper as previously described, or if you have made and experimented with the *camera obscura* (page 25), you have seen how you obtain an inverted image of the scene. In other words, the lens turns everything upside down.

How is the eye like a camera's lens?

In many ways, our eyes act like a camera. Let us examine the camera first so that we can better understand how our eyes work.

In a camera there are four basic parts

or controls. First, there is the lens itself; the light rays pass through it to form the image on the film. Second, there is the film, a special material sensitive to light, which produces the picture when it is developed in chemicals. Third, there is a control that varies the amount of light that passes through the lens, thereby providing just the right amount of exposure for the film. Finally, the distance regulator varies the distance between the lens and film so that we can focus the camera and obtain the sharpest picture, depending upon the distance of the object from the camera.

If you look in the mirror, you see that your eye consists of a colored circle on a white background with a black circle in the center. The colored portion is the iris. The black center is the pupil, an adjustable opening behind which is the eye's lens. The light passes through this lens and is focused on the curved back of the eyeball, or the retina, which acts like the film in a camera.

If you are in a dimly lit room, you'll find that the pupil is large, but in the bright sunlight, your pupil is small. The amount of light entering the eye through the pupil is controlled by the iris, which is a circular muscle. Too much light passing through the pupil would harm the retina, while too little would make it impossible to see.

We focus a camera to obtain a sharper image by changing the distance between the lens and film; the lens of the eye does not work in the same way. If you could look inside the eye, you would find several special muscles attached to the lens. These muscles control the shape of the lens which is convex. By changing the shape of the lens — making it thicker or thinner at the center — we are able to change the focal length of the lens and thus adjust for the distance of the object we are looking at.

There is seemingly an important difference between the eye and the camera. We know that the image produced by

HOW TO MAKE A SIMPLE TELESCOPE

To make a telescope you will need two convex lenses and two different sizes of cardboard tubing. The cardboard tubing should be such that the smallest size just fits within the larger one and can be moved back and forth easily.

If the opening of the cardboard tubing is much bigger than the lenses, cut a piece of heavy cardboard to the same size as the tube opening. Now place one of the lenses so that the center of the lens is exactly over the center of this cardboard disc. Trace around the edge of the lens and cut out the center of the cardboard disc carefully. Now tape the cut cardboard disc over the end of the tubing. Then tape the lens over the opening you have cut.

You are to repeat this for the other lens, attaching it to a cardboard disc which is placed on the second tubing size. The length of the tubing depends upon

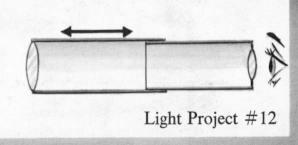

Light Project #12

the strength of the lenses you are using. It will be necessary to experiment with this, starting with each cardboard tube about 18 inches long, and cutting each down about 2 to 3 inches at a time.

You can determine the exact length by holding one lens in front of your eye and moving the inside tube back and forth until you see an enlarged image of the object you are looking at. Aim the tubes at an object about 10 or 15 feet away in order to determine the length of the tubes.

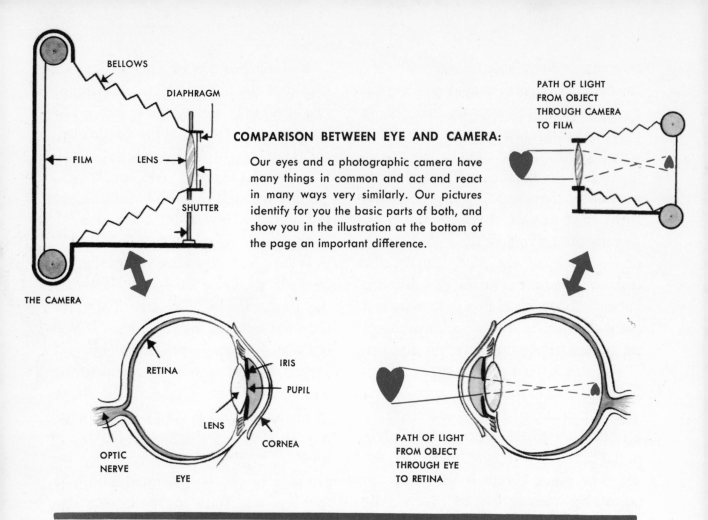

BELLOWS

DIAPHRAGM

FILM

LENS

SHUTTER

THE CAMERA

PATH OF LIGHT FROM OBJECT THROUGH CAMERA TO FILM

COMPARISON BETWEEN EYE AND CAMERA:

Our eyes and a photographic camera have many things in common and act and react in many ways very similarly. Our pictures identify for you the basic parts of both, and show you in the illustration at the bottom of the page an important difference.

RETINA

IRIS

PUPIL

LENS

CORNEA

OPTIC NERVE

EYE

PATH OF LIGHT FROM OBJECT THROUGH EYE TO RETINA

Just as in the camera, the object forms an inverted image on the retina of the human eye, but this image is turned right side up by the human mind.

the camera's lens is upside down. Yet, when we look at anything we see it right side up. You would no doubt ask if your eyes really invert the scene and produce an image that is upside down.

Actually, our eyes do produce an inverted image on the retina. However, knowing from experience that this is upside down, the image is adjusted by our brain which permits us to see things as they really are. This changing is solely the work of the mind which interprets what the optic nerve relays to it.

How much control our mind has over the interpretation of what our eyes see was demonstrated many years ago by a Swiss scientist. He tried an experiment in which several people wore special glasses. These glasses were convex lenses that turned the scene upside down just as the camera lens does. The eyes looking at the scenes upside down turned them right side up and this image was focused on the eye's retina. When the people first started to wear the glasses, they viewed everything right side up, but their brains, used to changing the message received from the eye's retina, inverted the scene. Thus, these people looked at the world upside down. However, after a few weeks of continually wearing these glasses, the mind, realizing that this was not the real world, suddenly accepted the images as they were received. The people wearing glasses saw everything right side up, just as if they were not wearing glasses. The mind adjusted to the changed situation. Then, when the glasses were removed, the mind, now taking the retina

image as true, caused these people without glasses to see things upside down. Again, after a short period of time, the mind readjusted and the people again saw normally.

Have your eyes regularly checked by a doctor. Lenses can correct faulty vision.

Why do people wear glasses?
When you look at an object in the distance, the lenses of your eyes form images on the retinas. As you move the object nearer, the shape of the lens must change or the image will be formed behind the retina. The muscles around the lens squeeze it so that it becomes more curved or thicker at the center.

If the eye muscles are too strong or not strong enough, or if the lenses are not properly shaped, the eye is unable to make the necessary changes in focus or *accommodation,* as it is called.

If the lens is too curved, the image then formed is in front of the retina. This condition is known as nearsightedness. On the other hand, if the lens is not curved enough, the image is formed behind the retina. This condition is known as farsightedness.

This condition of the eyes can be corrected by using another lens to aid the lens of the eye. The type of lens used in

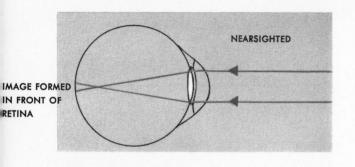

NEARSIGHTED

IMAGE FORMED
IN FRONT OF
RETINA

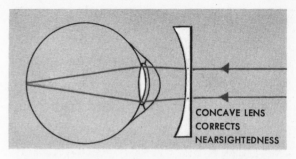

CONCAVE LENS
CORRECTS
NEARSIGHTEDNESS

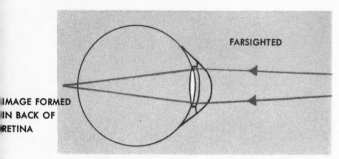

FARSIGHTED

IMAGE FORMED
IN BACK OF
RETINA

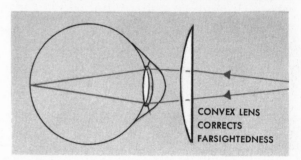

CONVEX LENS
CORRECTS
FARSIGHTEDNESS

Concave spectacle lenses correct nearsightedness; convex lenses help overcome farsightedness.

eyeglasses depends upon whether the person is nearsighted or farsighted and to what degree.

The light image that passes through the pupil and lens of the eye is transmitted to the brain by the optic nerve. The point at which this nerve is attached to the retina is not sensitive to light; it is known as the *blind spot*.

What is your "blind spot?"

You can find your own blind spot by using the accompanying blind spot test described below.

While we know that light travels very quickly, we must also remember that what we "see" is what our mind tells us we are looking at, and this involves more than the speed of light through the air. The light impulses received by the retina in the eyes are changed into nerve impulses and are transmitted to the brain by the optic nerves. These impulses also travel very quickly, taking a very small portion of a second to go from the eye to the brain. However, during that very small

What is an afterimage?

HOW TO MAKE THE BLIND SPOT TEST
Close your left eye and hold this page at arm's length so that the X is directly in front of your right eye. You'll see the circle out of the corner of your eye. While you continue to look at the X, move the page very slowly toward you.

Somewhere along the way, when the image of the circle is formed on the blind spot of your eye, the circle will disappear. Then as you continue to move the page closer and closer, it will reappear.

You will find the same is true of the star. It too will disappear, but at a distance closer to you.

Light Project #13

time interval, the eyes may have shifted to another scene. While the new impulses are picked up by the retina, the old ones are still traveling to the brain. Thus, our brain tells us we are seeing something different from what our eyes are actually looking at.

You can try this yourself by looking at the illustration above. Concentrate on the drawing for one or two minutes; then quickly turn your head so that you are looking at a clear blank wall. What do you see? You see the drawing on the wall. This is known as an *afterimage*.

An optical illusion is the name we use **Do your eyes ever betray you?** to describe something that we see with our eyes but which we know is not true. Remember earlier in this book the illusion of the full moon? It appeared bigger when it was just at the horizon than when it was high in the sky.

The accompanying illustrations include a number of the common optical illusions. These misinterpretations are due to a variety of causes, the most common of which are our lack of experience in viewing such scenes, carelessness and a physical timing factor.

The famous "which line is longer," is an example of carelessness, (See illustration, page 32). The upper line appears smaller because our eyes place the line's ends within the arrowheads rather than following the line to its tips.

Look at this diagram carefully and you will notice that where the white bands meet, shadows seem to flicker. It is an optical illusion created by the fact that any point away from the crossing of the white lines is surrounded by more black and looks brighter.

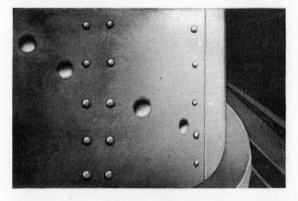

Turn the book upside down. How do the rivets and the dents appear now? Our eyes can fool us.

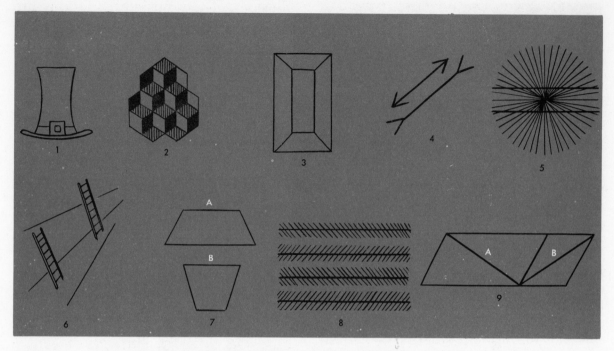

SOME MORE OPTICAL ILLUSIONS

Above are pictured a number of "famous" optical illusions. Test yourself and see how you score: 1. Is the hat as wide as it is high? 2. Count the cubes and then recount them carefully. 3. Look at the inside square; does it appear to shift back and forth? 4. Compare the length of the lines. Are they even in length? 5. Are the two horizontal lines curved or are they straight? 6. Which ladder is longer, or are they the same? 7. How does the length of lines A and B compare? 8. Are the horizontal lines parallel? 9. Compare the length of the diagonals A and B. Which one is longer or are they equal? Now take a ruler and measure to check your answers. Our eyes can fool us, as you can see.

Light and Color

What is "white light?" It was not until about 300 years ago that man began to unravel the mysteries of nature's colors. The experiments of the famous English scientist, Sir Isaac Newton, performed in 1665, are the basis for much of our knowledge of color. He found that when he passed a narrow beam of sunlight or "white light" through a triangular prism, the white light split into a multicolored beam. This colored beam, consisting of violet, indigo, blue, green, yellow, orange and red, is known as a *spectrum*.

Newton also discovered two other important facts about light and color. First, he found that he could not break any of the colors of the spectrum down into another group of colors as he had done with white light. He also found that he could pass the color spectrum through another triangular prism and produce white light. Thus, it was Newton who first discovered that white light is a combination of all the colors.

HOW TO MAKE A RAINBOW

The rainbow is nature's color spectrum. It always appears in one particular portion of the sky and only when you are facing away from the sun. The top of the rainbow is about halfway between the horizon and a point directly above your head. Furthermore, the sky behind the rainbow is always hazy or cloudy. It is the clouds or haze that make the rainbow possible.

The haze or clouds consist of millions of small drops of water and each of these drops acts as a prism breaking the reflected sunlight into a spectrum. Each drop reflects only a single color wave of the spectrum directly to our eyes, the color depending upon the height of the drop above the horizon.

You can make your own rainbow by placing a large piece of white paper on the floor in front of a window through which the bright sun is shining. Set a glass full of water on the window sill so that it extends slightly over the inside edge. The water in the glass will act as a prism and produce a spectrum on the paper on the floor.

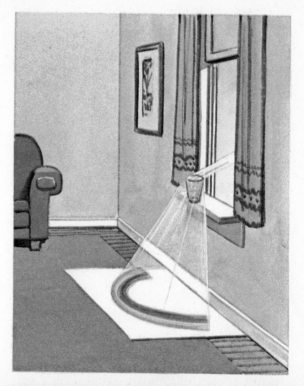

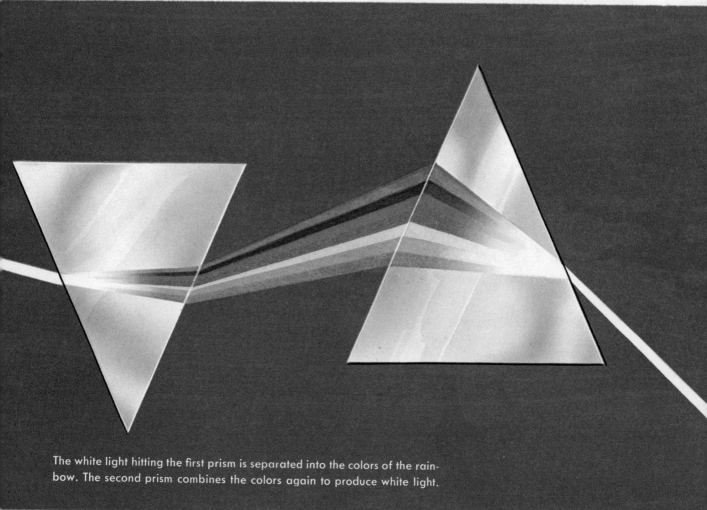

The white light hitting the first prism is separated into the colors of the rainbow. The second prism combines the colors again to produce white light.

When Newton first found that white light was composed of different colors,

How are white light and color related?

he believed that the colors were produced by different types of light "corpuscles" or "bullets." One type of bullet produced red light, another blue light, another green light, and so forth. His light theory became known as the corpuscular theory of light.

At about the same time that Newton lived, a Dutch scientist, Christian Huygens, was also studying light. It was he who originated the idea that light is a series of waves (much the same as those created by throwing a stone into a pond of water), with every point on a wavefront of light being a new source of wavelets and thus creating an indefinite number of wavefronts.

For many years, scientists studying light and color were divided into two groups; one group favored Newton's theory of light and the other favored Huygen's theory of light. However, there were some scientists who were not fully satisfied with either theory since neither could be proven true under all conditions. Many modifications of both theories were suggested, but none of these modifications was acceptable since scientists sought a theory that applied at all times under all conditions.

At the beginning of this book, in describing what is light, we noted that light is a form of energy that radiates in all directions from its source. This idea that light is a form of energy was formulated by the German scientist,

Max Planck in 1900 in his now famous *Quantum Theory.* He said that radiant energy such as light is composed basically of tiny irreducible bits of energy called *quanta* which travel or radiate from the light source.

Five years after Planck announced his theory, Albert Einstein proposed a more exact definition of the energy that causes light. While studying the composition of the atom, Einstein came to the conclusion that light, in spite of its wave nature, must be composed of an energy particle of the atom which he called a *photon.*

Today, despite the recognition of the greatness of the inventors of these various theories, scientists still are unable to decide upon a single theory of light. They accept the idea that light is a form

ern its behavior under certain conditions, but it will be up to the scientists of tomorrow — maybe one of you — to come up with the answer to: "What is light?"

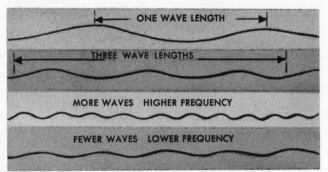

ONE WAVE LENGTH

THREE WAVE LENGTHS

MORE WAVES HIGHER FREQUENCY

FEWER WAVES LOWER FREQUENCY

PARTS OF A WAVE

of energy or radiation produced by the photon, but they also know that light travels like a wave. Thus, they accept the concept that light has two different disguises: first, when light travels from one place to another — from the sun to the earth or from an electric bulb to our eyes, or from an electric bulb to this page — the light travels as if it were a wave; secondly, when light is emitted by an object — such as light leaving the sun or leaving an electric bulb — or when light is absorbed by an object — such as a leaf taking in the light to produce its own food from carbon dioxide and water — the light acts as if it were a stream of "bullets" or photons.

Actually, no one today is certain exactly what light is. We know how it works and we have certain rules to gov-

What are the parts of a light wave?

To understand how a light wave travels and exactly what it is, it is best to study waves in water first, since you have all seen this kind of wave.

If you throw a pebble or stone into a pond or lake, it creates waves. The number of waves that comes to the shore varies, depending upon the size stone we throw into the lake. The number of waves, if measured for a specific period of time, say a minute, is known as *wave frequency*.

We can also study the length of the wave; that is, the distance from the crest (or top) of one wave to the crest of the next. This distance is known as *wave length*. Generally, the shorter the wave length the higher the frequency (greater the number of waves) and the longer the wave length the lower the frequency (fewer number of waves). Let's now apply this to the light waves.

35

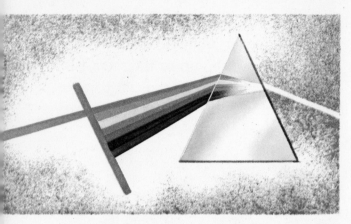

Color by absorption: The red glass plate absorbs practically all colors from the white light except the red, which passes through.

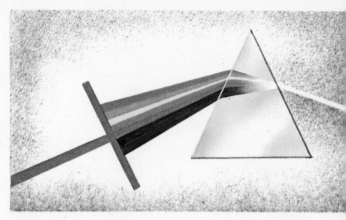

The blue glass plate absorbs practically all colors from the white light except the blue which passes through it unhampered.

Scientists have special instruments to

How long are light waves?

measure the length and frequency of the different color light waves found in the white light spectrum. This measurement is exceedingly fine work since the wave length of light is very, very small. As a yardstick for measurement, the scientists have created

Below, table of wave length of colors in the spectrum.

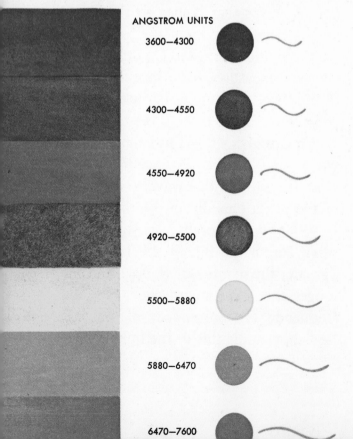

ANGSTROM UNITS

3600—4300

4300—4550

4550—4920

4920—5500

5500—5880

5880—6470

6470—7600

a special measuring unit; they call this unit of wave length the *angstrom*. One angstrom is equal to four billionths of an inch, or in other words, in one inch there are 250,000,000 angstrom units.

Studying the spectrum, scientists found that the wave length of red light is considerably longer than the wave length of violet light. The red light wave is 7,600 angstroms in length or about $\frac{28}{1,000,000}$ (twenty-eight millionths) of an inch. The violet light wave is about half as long or 4,000 angstroms or $\frac{16}{1,000,000}$ (sixteen millionths) of an inch. The wave lengths of the other colors of the spectrum vary between these two extremes, getting shorter when going from red to orange to yellow to green to blue to indigo to violet.

Applying our knowledge of the relation of lengths and frequency in water waves, we can readily see that the longer wave lengths have lower frequencies than the shorter wave lengths. Thus, violet light has a higher frequency than any of the others, and red light has a lower frequency than any of the others.

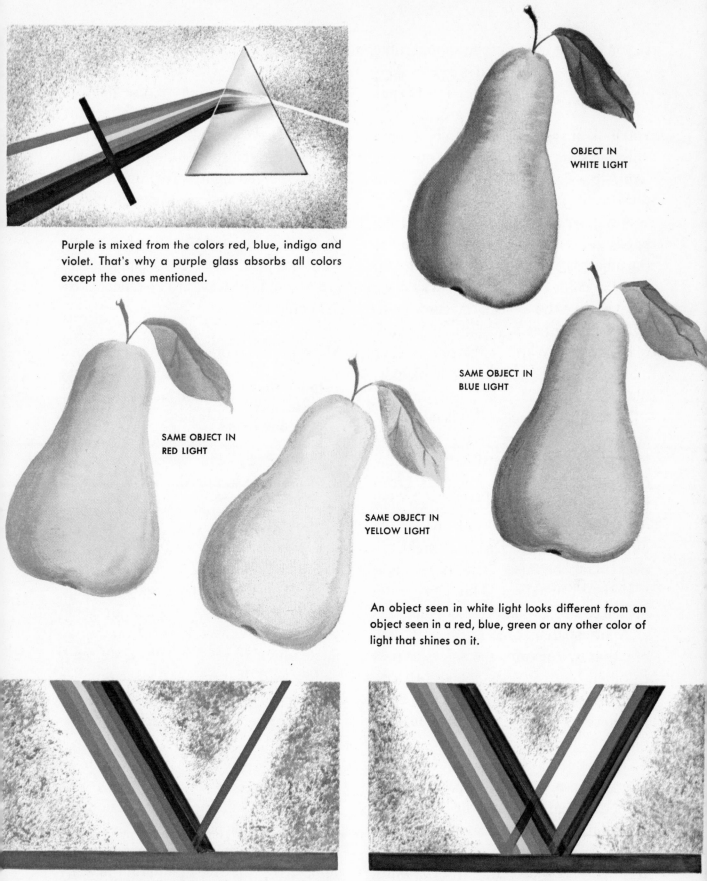

Purple is mixed from the colors red, blue, indigo and violet. That's why a purple glass absorbs all colors except the ones mentioned.

OBJECT IN WHITE LIGHT

SAME OBJECT IN RED LIGHT

SAME OBJECT IN YELLOW LIGHT

SAME OBJECT IN BLUE LIGHT

An object seen in white light looks different from an object seen in a red, blue, green or any other color of light that shines on it.

Colors by reflection: A blue surface will absorb practically all colors and reflect only blue.

The purple surface will absorb all colors and reflect only red, blue, indigo and violet.

If you look at a tree in the summertime

Why does an object have color? during the daytime, its leaves look green. But if you look at the same tree at night, with only the stars above and with no other light, the leaves will look black (see illustrations, pages 36-37).

Actually, the color of any object depends upon two things: (a) whether the object is opaque or transparent, and (b) the color of the light in which we are viewing the object. According to scientists, neither white nor black are really colors. White is the presence of all the colors of sunlight, while black is the lack of color.

An opaque object will reflect certain colors and will absorb the rest. The leaves on the tree we observed in the daylight in the summer appear green because the leaves reflect the green light waves of the sunlight and absorb the other colors. Those leaves at night appear black because there is no light that they can reflect. This lack of reflected colors is what produces black.

A transparent object transmits colors; that is, it permits the colors to pass through. Since it does not absorb certain colors and reflect others, it is clear and appears without any color, like ordinary window glass.

Translucent objects, on the other hand, diffuse the light waves that pass through them. We see the "color" of these objects on the basis of what type of light waves they permit to pass through and which they absorb. Thus, translucent objects can appear frosty or

without color like plain glass, or they can have color.

Similarly, the color of the light in which we view an object will affect the color of that object. If we look at a ripe red apple in the sunlight, that apple will reflect the red light waves and absorb the others; thus, we say the apple is red. But if we looked at the same apple under a blue lamp bulb, the apple would appear to be black since there are no red light waves to be reflected by the apple.

Many of the colors we see around us are

Can objects reflect more than one color? produced by paints or dyes. A tie is red because a special dye has been used to reflect the red light waves either from the sun or the standard white household electric bulb.

However, these dyes and paints do not produce pure natural colors as found in the white light or sunlight spectrum. A yellow painted wall in white light will reflect some green or some yellow light waves. If most of the reflected light waves are yellow, we see a yellow wall. If there are a large number of green light waves mixed in with the yellow light waves, we see a yellow-green wall.

Similarly, if you have ever mixed water colors or paints, you have found that if you combine equal portions of blue and yellow pigment, you will make a green color. What happens when sunlight strikes the green paint on the wall? The blue paint will absorb the yellow

38

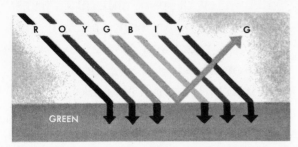

Green watercolors, consisting of mixed blue and yellow, reflect only green lightwaves, as the blue rays are absorbed by the yellow paint and the yellow by the blue paint parts.

light waves and the yellow paint will absorb the blue light waves (in addition to other colors), but since neither absorbs the green light waves, they will be reflected and you will see the green wall.

At one time it was believed that **Why is the sky blue?** the air was a blue gas and that was why the sky looked blue. Many other theories were advanced for the color of the sky, none of which was acceptable. Scientists sought an answer and they found it by studying smoke coming out of a chimney.

If you watch fine smoke rising into the air on a cloudy day, you will find that the smoke looks blue as it passes in front of a dark background. Make sure you are watching fine thin smoke against a darkened sky or you may not be able to see the blue.

This was the scientists' clue. The light reaching the smoke, which consists of many tiny particles of carbon, dust, unburnt fragments and other materials, was partially broken up by those particles. The blue light waves, which are exceedingly short, are bounced off by the particles, whereas the other colored light rays continue unaffected. The bouncing off, both as reflection and re-

In the light of the flashlight, water with milk in it will appear blue.

fraction, of the short blue light waves makes the smoke look blue.

The air about the earth is composed of many tiny particles, including dust and water vapor. As the sunlight passes through the air, the shorter blue light waves are reflected and refracted by the particles while the other colored light waves, being longer, are unaffected and are not reflected by the water vapor or dust in the air.

The blue waves spread all over the sky so that it appears blue. Here is a simple project to let you prove that fine particles will bend the blue light waves.

All you need for this project is a transparent water glass, water, a few drops of milk and a flashlight.

Pour a few drops of milk into a transparent glass filled with water. If you want to be exact and have an eye dropper, drop about 10 to 15 drops of the milk into the water. This milky-water is similar to the air above the earth that contains water vapor and dust.

Pull down the shades or put out the light in the room so that it is dark. Now, set your flashlight about one to two inches from the glass so that it is at right angles to the side of the glass. Turn the flashlight on. The water looks blue! The milk in the water has bent the blue light rays which are in the white beam of light from the flashlight, just as the moisture and dust bend the blue light rays coming from the sun.

HOW TO MAKE A COLOR WHEEL

From our study of color we know that white is the presence of all the colors of the spectrum. Here is a simple color wheel to help you prove this scientific observation.

Cut a circle of cardboard about 3 to 4 inches in diameter and divide it into six parts as shown in the diagram. Use water colors, paints or crayons to fill in the colors as indicated.

Set a small nail through the center, gluing it in place. When it is thoroughly dried, set the nail into a hand-drill as shown so that the disc can turn freely. Holding the drill so that you can watch the disc, turn the drill quickly until all the colors blend. Because there are many different types of drills, it is impossible to tell you exactly how fast to turn it. You will have to experiment. When you reach the right speed, all the colors will blend together and it will appear as if a white disc is at the end of the drill. Make certain that the drill you use can reach a very high speed when you are turning.

Light project #14

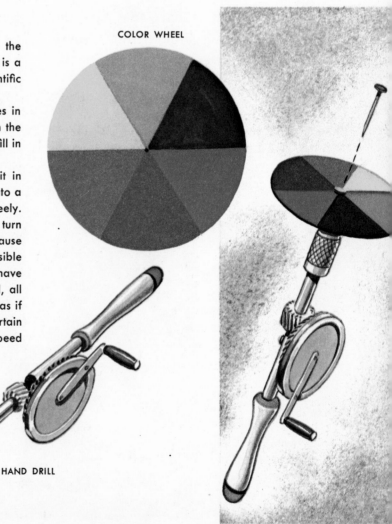

COLOR WHEEL

HAND DRILL

Polarized Light

One of the properties of light, according to scientists, is its traveling in wave form as it goes from one place to another. The

What are polarized light waves?

light from a source travels as a series of crests and troughs much like a wave in water. We can create such waves with a piece of string or rope. If you tie one end of the string to a door knob and hold the other end in one hand, you will be able to produce a wave by moving your wrist up and down. This type of wave, moving up and down, is known as a *vertical transverse wave* because it vibrates in a vertical plane, an imagi-

nary vertical surface. On the other hand, if you move your wrist from side to side, you will produce another type of a wave; it is known as a *horizontal transverse wave,* vibrating in a horizontal plane. Now, still holding the rope,

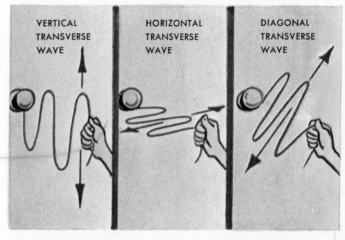

Like the waves in a string made by moving your wrist in all directions, light waves flow in different planes.

you can move your wrist along a diagonal — to the right as you go up and to the left as you go down. You have now produced another type of a wave different from either the vertical or horizontal transverse wave.

We know that light travels as a wave from place to place. But what kind of a wave is it? Actually, the light wave scientists talk about is a combination of several types of waves. It travels as a horizontal transverse wave, a vertical transverse wave and many types of diagonal transverse waves. In effect, it is a combination of waves each flowing in a different plane. If we isolate or separate any of these waves, that is, single out one wave in a given plane, we have polarized the light wave.

We have learned that light is transmitted by waves that travel horizontally, vertically and transversely. When a light ray passes through a polarized lens, part of the waves are blocked out, reducing the quantity of light. If we now pass what was left through a second polarized lens which is turned at 90° to the first one, no light at all will pass. In the illustration on page 41, you can create waves in the string. These waves move freely in all directions. In the illustration on this page, the slit in the box allows only vertical waves. If you turn the box 90°, only the horizontal motion is possible. If you combined two boxes, one with a horizontal slit and one with a vertical slit, you would find that no wave motion at all would reach the doorknob.

string through a vertical slit, as between the slats of a chair back or a specially cut cardboard box (see illustration). If you move your wrist up and down, the transverse wave produced will pass through the slit in the chair back and reach the door knob. However, what if you moved your wrist from side to side? You will create a horizontal transverse wave, but that wave will stop when it reaches the slit in the chair. You have just polarized the horizontal wave; you have stopped it from passing through the chair back while the vertical wave could pass through.

Similarly, we can do the same thing with light waves by using special materials or lenses. These materials consist of millions of small crystals shaped like needles and they permit only those light waves which vibrate in their direction to pass through the material. The material used is known as a *polarized plate* or *lens*.

Normally, polarized plates or lenses are used in pairs. When the two special lenses are placed so that their "slits" are

Let us return to the string for a moment

How can a wave be polarized?

to demonstrate another effect that would make it easier to understand light wave polarization. Suppose you leave the string tied to the door knob, but you now pass the

parallel, they let through only those waves that are in the same plane. When the slits are crossed or placed at right angles, they permit no light to pass through.

Actually, light is being polarized all

Why do we polarize light waves?

around us every day. It is polarized when sunlight is reflected and refracted by moisture and dust in the air and when light is reflected from very smooth non-metallic surfaces which act as mirrors. However, our eyes cannot tell the dif-

ference between polarized and non-polarized light waves. Yet, when we take photographs and want to eliminate unwanted reflections, such as the reflection from the glass in a picture frame, we use polarizing lenses to do this job. Similarly, when we are observing an object under a microscope, we can eliminate the unwanted reflections which may occur. Again, we use polarizing lenses to do the job. Similarly, polarized glass used in windshields of automobiles and motorboats reduces the glare from the sun and from the headlights of approaching vehicles.

The Speed of Light

It was not until man began to explore

Why did scientists measure the speed of light?

the universe with telescopes that he began to consider the question of the speed of light.

The renewed interest in science late in the sixteenth century resulted in men beginning to look for the answers to how and why. Scientists started to discover the speed of light because they were curious. They knew that you saw lightning before you heard thunder. They knew that sound traveled slower than light. But they wanted to know how fast did sound travel, how fast did light travel. The seeking of the answers to these and many other questions has always been the sign of a scientist.

In the early seventeenth century, the

How was the speed of light first measured?

famous Italian scientist, Galileo, tried to measure the speed of light as it traveled from a lantern on a hilltop a mile away from where he stood. The inadequacy of his timing instruments made it impossible for him to measure the speed of light accurately over so short a distance. Today, with our knowledge of the speed of light, we know that Galileo would have required a timing instrument that could measure less than one hundred thousandth of a second — that is the time light needs to travel one mile.

About fifty years after Galileo's experiment, the Danish astronomer, Ole Römer, in 1676, measured the speed of

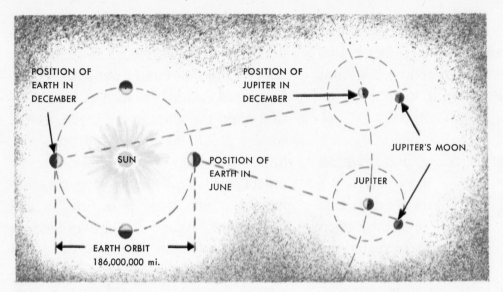

POSITION OF
EARTH IN
DECEMBER

POSITION OF
JUPITER IN
DECEMBER

JUPITER'S MOON

SUN

POSITION OF
EARTH IN
JUNE

JUPITER

EARTH ORBIT
186,000,000 mi.

The Danish astronomer Ole Römer measured the speed of light by observing the eclipses of one of the twelve moons of the planet Jupiter.

light by observing one of the eleven moons of the planet Jupiter. He assumed that light, like sound, traveled at a specific speed. It was known that the moons of Jupiter travel at a set speed around the planet and that it would take one of the moons 42½ hours to revolve around Jupiter, or in other words, that every 42½ hours it would be eclipsed by (disappear behind) the planet. He could make a time schedule of the eclipses for the entire year. But he had made his first observation in June, when Jupiter is nearest to the earth, and he found out in December, when Jupiter is farthest from the earth, that his schedule was off by 1000 seconds. (His schedule was 1000 seconds behind in December.) Römer knew that the distance across the orbit of the earth was 186,000,000 miles. He explained his schedule being off 1000 seconds by concluding that it took the light 1000 seconds to travel 186,000,000 miles, or 186,000 miles in one second. At that speed, if light could bend around the earth, it would circle the earth 7½ times in one second.

As scientists learned more about the

What is the speed of light?

universe and developed more precise measuring instruments, they made many attempts to measure the speed of light more precisely. One of the most famous of these experiments was conducted by the American scientist, Albert A. Michelson, in 1902. He used a precision machine and measured the speed of light as it traveled to and bounced back from a mirror that was 22 miles away.

The light traveled that distance in less than a thousandth of a second. He was able to make the measurements because his distance was greater and his instruments more precise than those which Galileo used almost 300 years before him. Michelson determined the speed of light at 186,284 miles per second.

It is interesting to note that the Michelson speed was less than one percent different from that of Römer,

The light waves are only a small part of the electromagnetic spectrum.

which was calculated with much poorer instruments some 225 years earlier. Scientists have conducted many additional experiments to measure the speed of light using different methods. On the average, these have shown that light travels at 186,282 miles per second.

We use the speed of light as a measuring stick in studying the universe. Some of the distances from earth are small enough that we can talk about them in miles. For example, the moon is about 240,000 miles away from the earth; the sun is about 93,000,000 miles away from the earth.

How long is a "light year?"

However, when we begin to measure distances to the stars, we find that we have to work with very large numbers. Just as scientists developed a special unit of measurement for the wave lengths of the different colors, so have scientists developed a special unit for measuring distance in space. It is a *light year*.

A light year is the distance that light travels in a single year. This is a large number considering that light travels about 186,000 miles per second. A light year is roughly 6,000,000,000,000 (six trillion) miles. Alpha Centauri, the nearest brilliant star, is more than 4 light years away.

Rays Other Than Light

Again we must return to the basic question: what is light? As you recall, scientists now believe that light is a form of energy that radiates waves in all

What is the "electromagnetic spectrum?"

directions. Let us pause for a moment to consider one essential word, "radiates."

Have you ever walked into the sunlight after being in the cool shade? Even if you had your eyes closed so that you

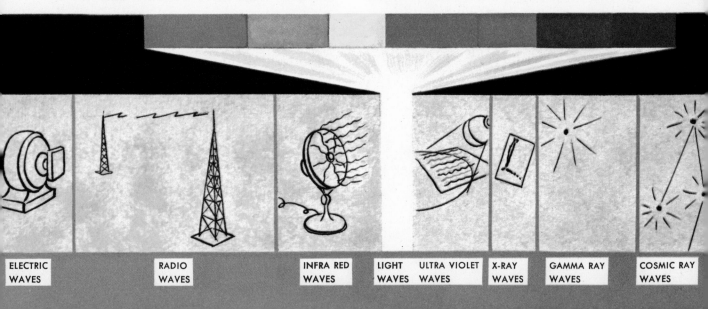

| ELECTRIC WAVES | RADIO WAVES | INFRA RED WAVES | LIGHT WAVES | ULTRA VIOLET WAVES | X-RAY WAVES | GAMMA RAY WAVES | COSMIC RAY WAVES |

could not see the sun, you would still know you were in the sunlight. Why? You would "feel" the sun since it would warm your body. But instead of walking into the sunlight, suppose you walked near a burning fire. Again you would "feel" the fire even if you did not see it. The fire, like the sun, is "radiating" heat, which is a form of energy.

Actually, we are continually surrounded by radiations. The sun is constantly bombarding the earth with cosmic rays, a form of radiation. The fire in the stove, the electric iron with which we iron clothes, the incandescent electric bulb by which we read — all are emitting heat, a form of radiation. Radio and radar, which we use to send and receive messages during the day or night, in clear weather or in fog, use a special type of radiation. Even the electricity we use in our homes is a form of radiation.

Scientists have put all the many types of radiations into a single category which they have labelled the *electromagnetic spectrum.*

The electromagnetic spectrum consists of waves whose wave lengths — the distance from the crest of one wave to the crest of the next — are over 20 miles long to wave lengths smaller than a billionth of an inch. We find that the very long waves are those radiated by electricity and radio transmitters, while the very short ones, the cosmic rays, are those radiated by the sun. Those with longer wave lengths have a lower frequency than those with shorter wave lengths.

What is the "visible spectrum?" That portion of the electromagnetic spectrum (or all forms of radiation) that we are able to see, is known as the *visible spectrum.* Light waves as a form of radiation are the only part of the electromagnetic spectrum that we can see with our eyes.

The visible spectrum extends from the red wave lengths, which are the longest of the visible spectrum, to the violet wave lengths, which are the shortest of the visible spectrum.

What are light's neighbors in the electromagnetic spectrum? Heat rays, the warmth we receive from the sun or from a fire, are part of the electromagnetic spectrum. These rays were identified by the famous English scientist, Sir William Herschel, about 1800. He found that these waves had longer wave lengths than red light; these waves are known as infra-red rays or waves. The prefix *infra* means below in Latin; infra-red rays are below red light waves in the electromagnetic spectrum—they have longer wave lengths and lower frequencies.

Shortly after Sir William Herschel reported his finding of infra-red rays, a German chemist, Johann Wilhelm Ritter, discovered special waves or rays at the other end of the visible light spectrum. These are known as *ultra-violet rays* or waves. The prefix *ultra* means beyond in Latin; ultra-violet rays are beyond the violet light waves — they have shorter wave lengths and higher frequencies than violet light waves.

As we increase the temperature of an object, it will radiate heat. If we increase the temperature high enough, the object will not only radiate heat but it will also radiate light waves. We use this scientific information in our everyday life since this is how the ordinary household electric light bulb works. There is a very fine wire inside the glass shell and we increase its temperature by sending electricity (also a form of radiation) through the wire. The wire becomes very hot and radiates heat and light. The same is true if we placed a piece of iron in a very hot fire. First, the iron would become too hot to touch. If we provided enough heat (and this varies depending upon the object we use), it will eventually glow with a red light.

How can we take photographs without light?

We use infra-red rays in many ways. In industrial plants, for example, special infra-red bulbs dry paint on automobiles quickly. We also have photographic film that is sensitive only to infra-red waves. This film is very useful in photographing on cloudy, misty days since the infra-red and red waves pass through the haze and mist more easily than the other visible waves. It is possible, by using this special film, to take a picture in complete darkness using two hot objects that emit infra-red waves that will be reflected by the subject which is being photographed.

When we heat any substance, such as the filament in an electric bulb, it will emit light. It is, possible however, to make a body emit light without being heated. Certain materials will emit light or "fluorescence" if exposed to ultra-violet waves. The English scientist, George Stokes first detected this phenomenon about 1850. It was his discovery that eventually resulted

What is "fluorescence?"

WHAT IS "BLACK LIGHT?"

We have used knowledge of fluorescence and ultra-violet light waves to produce a special light. When we fill a tube like the one used for fluorescent light with a special chemical, mercury, we find that this tube will emit both visible and ultra-violet light waves. If the tube is surrounded by a special glass that absorbs the visible light, only the ultra-violet light comes through. This we have called *black light*. Ultra-violet rays and black light are also used to sterilize milk and to keep meat stored in a refrigerator from spoiling.

Black light can be used to detect fingerprints which are not visible to the human eye in ordinary visible light. If you treat the prints with a fluorescent powder and expose them to black or fluorescent light, they will show up clearly.

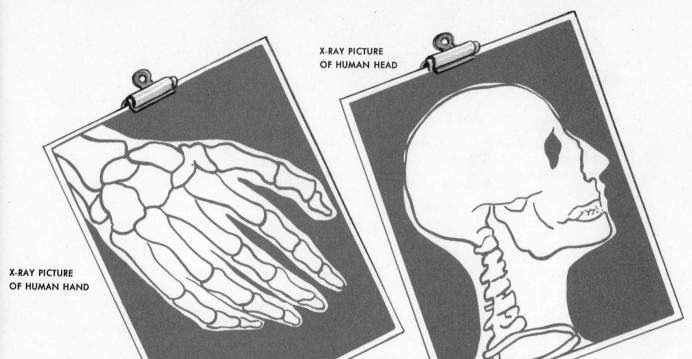

X-RAY PICTURE OF HUMAN HEAD

X-RAY PICTURE OF HUMAN HAND

in the development of the fluorescent tube and flourescent lighting which is used in homes and buildings. The inside of the glass tube is covered with a special material and the tube itself filled with a special gas. The electricity causes a spark which "shoots" through the gas in the tube, and the waves radiated by the gas cause the materials coated on the surface of the tube to fluoresce or emit light waves.

There are waves other than light waves

What are X-Rays?

that will pass not only through our bodies but even through heavy steel. These waves are thousands of times shorter than the shortest visible light rays and have much higher frequencies, somewhere near a billion billion waves per second.

These special waves were discovered by a German scientist, Wilhelm Roentgen, in 1895. In studying the waves emitted by a cathode ray tube, he found waves that would darken photographic

film just as visible light waves do. He also discovered that these waves would make materials fluoresce just as ultraviolet waves do. He called them *X-rays* because in mathematics, *x* stands for an unknown quantity.

Today these rays or waves are known as X-rays or Roentgen rays. The X-ray spectrum consists of a group of waves of varying wave lengths. The longer of these, known as "soft X-rays," can penetrate only soft substances, such as flesh, and are used to photograph bones or organs in the body. The shorter wave length X-rays, known as "hard rays," can penetrate thick, dense substances, such as iron or steel, and are used in industry to examine large metal machine parts for possible hidden cracks.

Light rays — radiation — observed since man is on earth, has still not yielded all its secrets. With the beginning of the space age and the research of cosmic and atomic radiation, we might be able to get closer to the answer of: What is light?